THE WILL OF GOD

IS

THE WORD OF GOD

D0874294

COMPANION GUIDE

THE WILL OF GOD
IS
THE WORD OF GOD

JAMES MACDONALD

B&H
PUBLISHING GROUP

NASHVILLE, TENNESSEE

978-1-4336-5029-1

Published by B&H Publishing Group
Nashville, Tennessee

Dewey Decimal Classification: 231.5
Subject Heading: GOD—WILL \ CHRISTIAN LIFE \
PROVIDENCE AND GOVERNMENT OF GOD

1 2 3 4 5 6 7 8 • 21 20 19 18 17

CONTENTS

Introduction   1

Chapter 1: Who Needs God's Will   7

Chapter 2: God's Will from God's Word   15

Chapter 3: God's Exact Will for Me, Now?   23

Chapter 4: Does God Have Specifics for Me?   31

Chapter 5: A Wonderful Freedom   39

Chapter 6: A Serious Accountability   47

Chapter 7: Decision Time—Part One   55

Chapter 8: Decision Time—Part Two   63

Conclusion   71

INTRODUCTION

The will of God is one of the most important things for a Christian to understand. Sadly, it is one of the most distorted doctrines of the church today. Too many Christians have bought into a view of God's will that leaves them helpless, hopeless, and confused. Christians are hurting because they think they've missed out on God's will—they've gotten off track and will never be able to get back.

Have you ever felt like this? Maybe you think you chose the wrong college or the wrong major. Maybe you think you think you chose the wrong type of schooling for your children or moved to the wrong neighborhood. Maybe your marriage is no longer happy and joyful, so you think you've married the wrong person. Or maybe you're paralyzed about an upcoming decision. Should you take a new job, or keep the one you have? Should you major in management or social work? Should you buy a house now, or wait for the economy to change? Making decisions is difficult, and we all struggle with regret. No wonder it's so easy to believe we've missed God's will!

But the Bible gives us great news about God's will. When we study the Bible to understand God's will, we don't learn about some strange, mysterious process of decision-making. We don't learn that God has a secret agenda, and that we have to play our cards just right to figure it out. We don't learn that one bad mistake can derail us, causing us to miss out on God's will for the rest of this life. The Bible tells us God's will is not a hidden or mysterious reality that we must seek to identify. Rather, the Bible IS God's will. In it, He tells us everything we need to know for life and godliness.

By working through this companion guide and reading *The Will of God* IS *the Word of God*, I pray you will begin to understand God's will for your life and live in obedience to Him. May He bless you as you read and may you feel the peace and freedom that comes from knowing God is not a grumpy micromanager, but a loving Shepherd whose Word to you *IS* His will for you!

How to Use This Book

This workbook is a companion guide to *The Will of God* IS *the Word of God*. Each chapter in the workbook is consistent with the same chapter in the book. You'll want to read the chapter in the book first, and after each chapter, work through the same chapter in the workbook.

In this workbook, you'll find several questions in each chapter to help you process your thoughts and reactions. You'll also find some commentary and Scripture to help you think through what you're learning about God's will, as well as a prayer at the end of each chapter.

You'll notice there is a good bit of room between each question. That space is for you! Write out your answers to each question, the insights you're gaining, the pushback you might be feeling, the difficulties of having your views challenged, or even prayers that God would help you submit to His Word. This workbook is for you, so feel free to express yourself in response to the questions.

By Yourself

You're welcome to go through this workbook by yourself or in a group, though I recommend that, even if you go through it individually, you have someone to talk to about God's will for your life. It is easy to convince ourselves that God wants us to do something when we're not talking to anyone else; it often takes a good friend to keep our thoughts in check! This is why church involvement is so important for the Christian. Every Christian should be active in a local church where individuals come together to learn and obey God's will by studying his Word.

If you decide to go through the companion guide by yourself, you make the rules! There are only two important things to remember: First, make sure to read one chapter at a time and then come to the workbook, rather than reading two or three at a time or jumping around out of order.

Second, be honest! It can be very difficult to have our views about God challenged, and I suspect many of you will as you read this book. Be honest with yourself and with God. There's no shame in having misunderstandings about God's will; the problem occurs when we're unwilling to reshape our understanding by submitting to God's Word. Don't rush through the hard things. Take your time and work it out by writing out your responses and reactions to the questions.

With a Group

You may find it helpful to work through this book in a one-on-one discipling relationship or in a small group—that's great too.

It's best to meet once a week at a set time in a set place. Make sure everyone makes a commitment to read the content each week and show up prepared. Commit to reading one chapter on your own each week, answering the questions in this workbook, and coming to the group prepared to discuss what God is teaching you.

Again, honesty is key! The most successful group studies are those where the whole group is willing to be honest and vulnerable with God and with one another. Again, there's no shame in having misunderstandings about God's will! The important thing is that you are willing to submit to his Word and to engage with other Christians honestly.

Ephesians 5:19–21 calls Christians to "speak to one another in psalms, hymns, and spiritual songs . . . give thanks always for everything to God the Father . . . and submit to one another in the fear of Christ." Hebrews 10:25 tells us not to "neglect to gather together . . . but encourage each other." We must remember these important commands when we gather with our brothers and sisters. Jesus doesn't want us to be a bunch of individual Christians out doing our own things; He wants us to meet together, encourage one another, pray for one another, sharpen one another, and bear one another's burdens! Keep these things in mind as you gather with your group.

As a Supplement

This book is meant to be a supplement to your Bible reading and prayer. It should by no means replace time that you are spending in God's Word, but should foster a greater desire to spend time in the Word. The basic presupposition of this book is that God's Word (the Bible) is His will, and that He shapes us, primarily, as we read His Word. Thus, if this study draws you away from time reading the Bible, it has defeated its own purpose!

In addition, this book should not lead you away from prayer. At the end of each chapter, you'll find a prayer. As you're processing what you learn about God, His will, and His Word, talk to Him about it! He is your loving Father and has your best interest in mind. He wants to hear from you. Take time, whether you work through this study individually or in a group, to pray at the end of each chapter.

It is often easy to skip over the prayer section of books like this to get to the "important stuff." We want to think about God, read about Him, and see how what He says applies to our lives, but do we really want to talk to Him? To know Him? To spend time in His presence? Just as God changes us through His Word, he changes us through prayer. So don't rush past the prayer section in each chapter, and don't let this study take time away from your regular prayer. Work out what you're learning, struggling with, and wrestling with through prayer.

In the meantime, I'd like to pray for you as you begin this journey.

A Prayer

Heavenly Father,

Thank You for your goodness and Your grace. Thank You for revealing Yourself to us in Your Word. Thank You that all Your plans work together for Your glory and for the good of Your children. Thank You for Your love.

I pray for each person who reads this book and works through this workbook. Bless them, Father, by revealing Yourself to them through Your Word. May they grow in their awe of You, their love for You, and their obedience to You as they learn about Your will.

In Jesus' name, amen.

CHAPTER 1

Who Needs God's Will

1. Jot down some of the primary things you have been taught about God's will.

_____

_____

_____

_____

_____

_____

_____

2. Pages 2–7 included a quiz and answer key. How did you score on the quiz? What was your response to the answer key? Were there any beloved teachings challenged for you in this chapter?

_____

_____

_____

_____

_____

3. What emotions does reading about God's will stir up in you?

_____

_____

_____

_____

_____

_____

Discussing God's will can instigate some serious emotional responses. This makes sense. After all, what's more important than knowing God's will for your life? As emotionally charged as this conversation can be, however, we must always submit to God's Word. We must bring our presuppositions about God's will to Him, always allowing His Word to confront us in areas where we might be wrong. If we have a misunderstanding about God's will—either about the specifics of His will or about the ways He reveals His will to us—we need to be open to letting the Scriptures correct us, no matter how tightly we hold our view.

4. Describe a time in your life when you longed to know God's will.

_____

_____

_____

_____

_____

_____

_____

_____

5. Describe a time in your life when you felt really confused about God's will.

_____

_____

_____

_____

_____

_____

_____

6. Do you think God wants us to know His will or that He hides from us? What light does Jeremiah 29:13 shed on this?

_____

_____

_____

_____

_____

_____

7. We considered three powerful motivations for studying God's will: because of widespread misunderstanding, abuse, and consternation. Which motivation(s) applies to you?

_____

_____

_____

_____

_____

8. What are some significant life choices you're facing on which you need and want to know God's will?

_____

_____

_____

_____

_____

_____

_____

_____

_____

9. Read and reflect on Matthew 7:24–27. If our goal is to build our lives upon solid truth, what rock-solid truths are you learning about God's will?

_____

_____

_____

_____

_____

_____

_____

Pursuing a greater understanding about God and His will can be a challenging and even troubling endeavor. Christians believe that God is the most important being in the universe, so when our understanding of who He is or how He operates is challenged, we often don't know how to respond. But take heart! I believe God's Word reveals His will to us, and if you will submit to His Word and allow it to shape your view of God's will, you will come out on the other side with greater love, respect, and admiration for the God who has revealed His will.

10. Write your own prayer of response to God incorporating some of the verses and themes of this chapter.

_____

_____

_____

_____

_____

_____

_____

_____

_____

Prayer

Heavenly Father,

For those who feel confused about Your will, I ask You for clarity.

For those who feel abused by human teaching about Your will, I ask You for healing.

For those who have abused the topic of Your will by using it as leverage, I ask You for honesty and repentance.

And for those who are flat-out frustrated and determined to understand Your will so they can obey it, I ask You for light, truth, and power.

Fill all of us with a growing desire to know and love You and to live out Your will.

In the name of Jesus, who came to give us abundant life, amen.

CHAPTER 2

God's Will from God's Word

1. In one sentence, summarize your understanding of God's sovereign will.

_____

_____

_____

2. In one sentence, summarize your understanding of God's moral will (hint: see the title of the book).

_____

_____

_____

3. What decisions have you made today (or will you face today) that are based on God's will (the Bible)?

_____

_____

_____

_____

_____

_____

4. Does God's will (the Bible) feel confining or freeing to you? Why?

_____

_____

_____

_____

_____

_____

God's sovereign will includes His settled, secret purposes that will surely come about. God's moral will is His written expectations for human behavior, which are completely detailed in the Bible. (p. 30)

At first, it can feel disappointing or even frustrating to learn that God's will for us is completely detailed in the Bible. It seems like a bit of a letdown to our finite human minds. We like to believe that God has some huge plan out there just waiting to be discovered by us. We also like to believe that God wants us to chase our dreams and do whatever it takes to realize them . . . even if it means disobeying what He has already revealed. The reality—one that sometimes feels confining to us—is that if pursuing our goals or chasing our dreams causes us to disobey God's Word, we are living squarely *outside* of His will. At that point, we're trying to put God's stamp of approval on our desires, while ignoring His desires.

5. God gives us the ability to make wise choices and honors our efforts to choose well. Describe a time when you got to make a choice between several equally good options.

_____

_____

_____

_____

_____

_____

6. When we pray the line **"your will be done"** (Matt. 6:10) in the Lord's Prayer, to which aspect of God's will are we referring—His sovereign will, His moral will (revealed in the Bible), or both? Why?

_____

_____

_____

_____

_____

7. Reread 1 Thessalonians 4:3 and then reflect on your life in the past three years. What growth have you experienced? In what ways is God sanctifying you?

_____

_____

_____

_____

_____

_____

_____

_____

_____

We will only desire to fully submit to God's will—the Bible—when we believe He has our best interests in mind. The reason we continually fall prey to the trap of searching for His will outside of His Word is that we don't really trust that He is on our side. Only when we taste and see His goodness and trust that He knows what's best for us will we fully submit to His will. And this requires a lot of refining work by the Holy Spirit.

8. How would you like to see God continue to refine you?

_____

_____

_____

_____

_____

_____

_____

_____

9. Write your own prayer of response to God incorporating some of the verses and themes of this chapter.

_____

_____

_____

_____

_____

_____

_____

_____

Prayer

Heavenly Father,

Thank You for creating me with a will of my own, for I am created in Your image. Thank You for assuring me that You are the sovereign King over the universe, and nothing thwarts Your purposes. You use all things to advance Your kingdom. Thank You for revealing Your will through Your Word. Thank You that it's Your will for me to be both saved and sanctified, and that for the rest of my life, You will continue to refine me. I want to live like I belong to You, because I do. Father, give me the joy You reserve for those whose lives belong entirely to You.

I yield myself and my will more completely to You, Lord, in the name of Jesus, my Savior and Redeemer, amen.

CHAPTER 3

God's Exact Will for Me, Now?

1. Has this chapter challenged any of your previously held impressions about God's will for your life?

_____

_____

_____

_____

_____

_____

2. What questions do you still have?

_____

_____

_____

_____

_____

3. Is it freeing to learn that God doesn't have a highly specific, individualized will for your life?

_____

_____

_____

_____

_____

4. In what ways is that discovery scary? How does the freedom of choice put more responsibility on your decision making?

_____

_____

_____

_____

_____

_____

> This "perfect will" teaching sounds holy, and it exalts the perfection of God's sovereign will. But if God's will for us is really that unknowable and undiscoverable, then we are just a single wrong choice away from total ruin. (p. 41)

If God were a weak God, out of control and responding to forces more powerful than Himself, this idea of His will would be terrifying! Fortunately for us, we worship the all-powerful, all-wise Creator of the universe who promises that all things will work together for our good. Because we worship this kind of God, the truth about His will should free us. It reminds us that we aren't "a single wrong choice away from total ruin." Rather, we can operate in the freedom He has given us, in submission to the Bible, and with confidence that He is in control.

5. Identify some issues on which you have sought God's will through prayer. What does God's Word actually say about those issues? If you are not violating God's Word, then what's keeping you from making an informed and thoughtful choice?

_____

_____

_____

_____

_____

_____

_____

6. Within the protection of God's Word, God lets you make choices. Describe a time when God allowed you to choose between two good options.

_____

_____

_____

_____

_____

_____

_____

7. Do you tend to perceive God more as a divine micromanager or as the tender Shepherd-Guide? Why?

_____

_____

_____

_____

_____

_____

_____

_____

8. What does it look and feel like to follow a Shepherd?

_____

_____

_____

_____

_____

_____

9. "God's will is about the kind of person you were, the kind of person you currently are, and the kind of person you can become" (p. 48). What kind of person does God want you to become?

_____

_____

_____

_____

_____

_____

_____

_____

10. Write your own prayer of response to God incorporating some of the verses and themes of this chapter.

_____

_____

_____

_____

_____

_____

_____

_____

_____

Prayer

Father God,

Thank You for being my Shepherd-Guide. Thank You for how You gently tend and lead me. So often I act like a sheep, hovering over the succulent grass You provided, continually looking back at You to ask, "Can I eat this? Can I chew on this blade of grass?" Please help me to have greater confidence in Your gifts and guidance.

Help me to live more fully the abundant life You provided for me through Your Son, Jesus Christ, in whose matchless name I pray, amen.

CHAPTER 4

Does God Have Specifics for Me?

Chapter 4 listed six blessings that flow from a biblical perspective on God's will:

- We can conform our beliefs to the teaching of Scripture. (p. 75)
- We can live free from anxiety and guilt about God's will. (p. 76)
- We can recognize the validity of equal options. (p. 78)
- We can challenge immature or unwise decisions of loved ones—and be open to having our own decisions challenged. (p. 79)
- We can avoid indecision. (p. 83)
- We can reduce subjectivity. (p. 86)

1. Of these six blessings, which did you find most encouraging? Why?

_____

_____

_____

_____

2. How did this chapter challenge your thinking about God's will?

_____

_____

_____

_____

_____

3. Read Psalm 1. How does this passage connect obeying God's Word to prosperity?

_____

_____

_____

_____

_____

_____

_____

4. Look back on some past decisions in your life. Which would you now view differently?

_____

_____

_____

_____

_____

5. Look forward to some pending decisions you need to make in your life. Write a list of upcoming choices.

_____

_____

_____

_____

_____

_____

_____

_____

_____

Having listed some of these pending decisions in your life, go back to Psalm 1. Read it again, slowly. Meditate on this psalm one word at a time. What does it look like, in your upcoming decisions, to delight in the law of the Lord? How can you avoid walking in the counsel of the wicked and sinners? What does the wisdom of God have to say to your pending decisions?

6. How does abandoning the concept of God's individual will for your life shift more direct responsibility to your choices?

_____

_____

_____

_____

_____

7. How open are you to having your life decisions lovingly challenged by wise advisors in your life? Who fills that role for you?

_____

_____

_____

_____

> When we start contriving some personalized, customized will of God that allows us to do what we want and then claim it is God's will, we isolate ourselves from the family of faith that is supposed to sound the alarm when we begin to get off course and away from God's Word. The "God's will" card may allow you to limit the pressure of true accountability, but it doesn't lead to sanctification or joy, which we do know *IS* God's will for us. (p. 82)

8. How does living in community prevent you from playing the "God's will" card and stamping God's approval on something He doesn't approve?

_____

_____

_____

_____

_____

_____

9. Write your own prayer of response to God incorporating some of the verses and themes of this chapter.

_____

_____

_____

_____

_____

_____

_____

_____

Prayer

Father God,

I am confident in Your ability to accomplish Your sovereign will. Nothing will undermine Your master plan. I commit myself to obeying Your Word. Thank You for those instructions for living. So I accept that I need not worry about a hidden plan for my life. Please help me to make wise decisions, to be committed to Your Word, to be open to hearing from Your people, and to trust that You can handle whatever I choose. Thank you for the challenge and freedom to serve You.

In the name of Jesus, my Savior and Master, I pray, amen.

CHAPTER 5

A Wonderful Freedom

1. Rather than treating biblical characters' lives as templates for our lives, how should we approach their stories?

_____

_____

_____

_____

_____

> What often matters most to us is our own lives. Becoming the people God wants us to be is relegated to the back burner. Too often we want God to get excited about our dreams and plans, confirming for us the car/house/person/job that makes us feel complete. But as we grow and mature in our faith, we learn that life isn't about God getting on our program; it's about us getting on God's program. (p. 102)

2. Consider how you phrase your prayer requests. When you pray, are you trying to get God on your program, or are you getting on God's program? Cite specifics.

_____

_____

_____

_____

_____

_____

_____

We must realize that God is not a means to our ends; we are a means to His. He calls us for the purpose of His mission: taking the gospel to every tribe, tongue, and nation. This is His program. Our prayers must be oriented toward getting on His program, rather than trying to get Him on ours.

3. How does God's sovereign will leave room for our individual choices?

_____

_____

_____

_____

_____

_____

4. What are some things in your life that you can't control?

_____

_____

_____

_____

_____

_____

_____

_____

_____

5. In your own words, describe the process of sanctification in your life.

_____

_____

_____

_____

_____

_____

_____

_____

_____

6. How well do you know God's will, as revealed in His Word?

_____

_____

_____

_____

If we really believe God's will *IS* His Word, we should seek to learn it as well as possible! Because the Bible reveals all we need to know for life and godliness, we must devote as much time and energy as possible to reading, meditating on, and memorizing His will as revealed in His Word.

7. Read Ephesians 5:15–17 again. In light of these verses, evaluate the last few decisions you've made. To what degree did you consider how your choices might please God?

_____

_____

_____

_____

_____

8. As you've read these chapters, how has your perception of God's will changed?

_____

_____

_____

_____

_____

9. Write your own prayer of response to God incorporating some of the verses and themes of this chapter.

_____

_____

_____

_____

_____

_____

_____

Prayer

Sovereign God,

My life is in Your hands. You know me, love me, and guide me. I want to be more diligent in knowing You, loving You, and following You. Thank You for the wisdom to make good choices. I want to please You, Lord, and to become the person You have called me to be.

Please continue Your sanctifying work in me through Your Holy Spirit, making me more like Your Son, Jesus Christ, my Savior and Lord, amen.

CHAPTER 6

A Serious Accountability

1. What are some gray areas in life—choices that aren't explicitly taught in Scripture? Do you have any decisions to make right now in one of these areas?

_____

_____

_____

_____

_____

_____

2. How would you define true wisdom?

_____

_____

_____

_____

_____

_____

3. How has this chapter deepened your understanding of wisdom?

_____

_____

_____

_____

_____

In Proverbs 4:11, Solomon encourages his son by telling him, "I have taught you the way of wisdom; I have led you in the paths of uprightness." It is important to note, he does not say to his son, "I reveal to you every decision you should make; I always tell you the right choices." God does not appear through the clouds to tell us everything we should do. Rather, as we submit to His Word and the Holy Spirit sanctifies us, He conforms us into the image of Jesus and leads us in the way of wisdom, so that we can make wise decisions.

4. Who in your life could offer you godly counsel—wise people who know God's Word and are willing to challenge you when needed?

_____

_____

_____

_____

5. Read and reflect on James 1:1–8. Does living wisely guarantee you an easy life? What clues do you find in the text?

_____

_____

_____

_____

_____

_____

_____

6. How does James describe the attitude of a person who prays an effective prayer for wisdom?

_____

_____

_____

_____

7. In contrast, what are the traits of a person who neither prays for wisdom confidently nor uses the wisdom that God provides?

_____

_____

_____

_____

8. How have you seen God sovereignly work something messy for your good?

_____

_____

_____

_____

_____

_____

_____

Just because the Bible doesn't clearly spell out some decisions doesn't mean God hasn't given us guidelines for our personal choices. A biblical approach to wise decision-making in matters of personal choice will involve certain steps. Knowing and taking these steps often transforms what at first seems to be a confusing problem into a clear decision. (p. 128–29)

9. Chapter 6 lists five steps for decision making: *Eliminate unbiblical options. Pray for God's wisdom. Yield to the Holy Spirit's leading. Weigh heavily the consensus of godly counsel. Trust God's sovereignty to use all wise decisions for your good.* On which of these steps do you need the most work?

_____

_____

_____

_____

_____

10. Write your own prayer of response to God incorporating some of the verses and themes of this chapter.

_____

_____

_____

_____

_____

_____

_____

_____

_____

_____

Prayer

Sovereign God,

You are in control, and You are good, so I can trust You. Always. All true wisdom flows from You (Prov. 9:10). Father, I love You, and I want to please You, and I know that desire in and of itself is pleasing to You. I know that my vision is limited, and I need Your wisdom to see and choose what's best. Please lead me to others who will speak wisdom into my life, too. Thank You that You promise to give me wisdom generously, and You always keep Your promises.

In Jesus' name I pray, amen.

CHAPTER 7

Decision Time—Part One

1. Describe a time when you made a really tough choice, and your primary motivation was to please God. How did that look and feel in the short-term? Over time, how did it play out?

_____

_____

_____

_____

_____

_____

_____

2. "Glory is what emanates from God. Glory is the weight of God's presence" (p. 152). Describe a time when you clearly saw God's glory, when you concluded in awe, "There is a God."

_____

_____

_____

_____

_____

3. What is a specific choice Jesus made that you, as a Christ-representative, want to emulate?

_____

_____

_____

_____

_____

4. Review your past choices. What choice did you make then that you realize now did not meet the "God check"?

_____

_____

_____

_____

_____

> It's not always right to do what is within your right to do. Others are involved. It doesn't necessarily help others if you're only interested in helping yourself. (p. 151)

5. Paul's encouragement to the Corinthian church to put the concerns of others before their own does not square well with our natural, selfish desires. What does it say about God that He would have us consider others' needs before our own?

_____

_____

_____

_____

_____

_____

_____

6. Do you tend to do the "God check" first, or do you treat God as an afterthought in the decision-making process? Give examples.

_____

_____

_____

_____

_____

_____

We mentioned in chapter 5's questions that our prayers need to be oriented toward us getting on God's program, rather than getting Him on our program. This applies here as well. If we treat God as an afterthought in our decision making, we are inadvertently telling Him that we know better than He does. If, on the other hand, we do the "God check" first, we are submitting to His wisdom. We are, as the psalmist says, "waiting for the LORD" (Ps. 27:14).

7. How can the perspective of standing before the judgment seat of Christ affect your choices?

_____

_____

_____

_____

_____

_____

8. Read and reflect on Matthew 11:25–30. How do the words of Jesus' prayer show that God's will isn't about a prescribed, booby-trapped plan but about an intimate relationship with God the Father?

_____

_____

_____

_____

_____

_____

9. Write your own prayer of response to God incorporating some
of the verses and themes of this chapter.

_____

_____

_____

_____

_____

_____

_____

_____

Prayer

My Father,

Thank You not only for revealing wisdom in Your Word but also for Your Son's "footprints" in the Gospels. I want to walk as Jesus walked. When I feel burdened by life's choices, I want to come to You and find rest for my soul. Teach me to live in that intimate relationship with You. Thank You for always walking ahead of me, beside me, and behind me every step of the way (Ps. 139:5).

In the name of the Lord Jesus and for Your glory alone, amen.

CHAPTER 8

Decision Time—Part Two

1. Review the three "boat check" questions. Which of these feels the most unfamiliar or challenging to you?

_____

_____

_____

_____

_____

_____

> You are not an island. In fact, your choices
> ripple out and affect those in proximity to you.
> If you want to make wise decisions, you have
> to consider the relational angle. (p. 164)

2. Describe a time when you made a choice based on the others in the boat, not just on your own desires.

_____

_____

_____

_____

_____

3. Can you think of a situation, like my flower box story, when a choice might technically be right but could appear wrong? Describe.

_____

_____

_____

_____

_____

_____

_____

4. Can you think of a situation, like the Corinthians' meat-eating scenario, when a choice might technically be right but might cause your spiritual siblings to stumble? Describe.

_____

_____

_____

_____

_____

_____

5. Read Philippians 2:5–11. What do you learn about Christ in this passage? What would it look like in your life to imitate Him by putting others before yourself?

_____

_____

_____

_____

_____

_____

_____

_____

_____

This is one of the most challenging and unattractive demands Jesus makes on His followers. In a world that knows no higher god than the god of personal freedom, this is quite a countercultural command! There might be things that you or I want to do that are morally justifiable, which might not cause us to sin against God, but will cause our brothers and sisters in Christ to stumble. We must remember in these moments that there would have been *nothing* wrong with Christ staying at the right hand of the Father. There would have been *nothing* wrong with Him deciding not to save us. He did not have to give up His power and privilege to save sinners; *but He did.* We must have the same mind-set, one that puts the needs and desires of others before our own preferences.

6. What is something potentially addictive or enslaving to you?

_____

_____

_____

_____

In our culture, we tend to think of addiction exclusively in terms of alcohol or drugs. It makes sense—we have a serious drug and alcohol problem in our country. But humans can be addicted to countless things that are unrelated to drugs or alcohol. It could be your cell phone, video games, food, the affirmation of others, achievements at work, good grades, and the list goes on! It's good to ask ourselves every now and then, "What in my life would I not be okay without?" The first couple things that pop into your mind could very well be addictions.

7. Describe a time when your personal convictions caused you to question whether or not something was right.

_____

_____

_____

_____

_____

_____

8. What are some commitments you have made and need to keep?

_____

_____

_____

_____

_____

9. The sequence is significant: God check, boat check, gut check. How do you tend to order the checks on your choices? Think back to a choice you made recently and how you arrived at that decision.

_____

_____

_____

_____

_____

_____

_____

_____

10. Write your own prayer of response to God incorporating some
of the verses and themes of this chapter.

_____

_____

_____

_____

_____

_____

_____

_____

_____

Prayer

Lord God,

Thank You for the freedom You've given me. It's scary, in a way; part of me wishes You had simply laid out a blueprint for my life. Making all these choices in life is a big responsibility. But because of the freedom You've given me, I can, in a meaningful way, please You. Thank You for that opportunity, Father, and help me to make wise choices that please You. Help me to develop the disciplines of thinking carefully through my choices in light of pleasing You, loving others, and honoring my own convictions and commitments. Teach me to keep my word, even when it hurts. Teach me to love others as I want to be loved. Open my eyes to see that being loving is always more important than being "right."

In Jesus' strong name I pray, amen.

CONCLUSION

We're at the end of the journey. You've survived eight chapters about God's will, and perhaps God has worked some changes in your views of Him and His will. I pray this book and workbook have helped you gain a greater, biblical understanding of God's will for your life. Remember, the will of God *IS* the Word of God!

There were some suggestions at the conclusion of the book, listed again below. At the close of this journey, take some time to reflect on each of these suggestions and write some things you sense the Spirit of God impressing upon you about how you can apply them to your life.

1. Believe and live every moment in the reality of God's abiding love for you.

_____

_____

_____

_____

_____

_____

2. Let's be gracious with those stuck in the old, unbiblical paradigm.

_____

_____

_____

_____

_____

3. Let's purpose afresh to spend more time in God's Word, feeding on and familiarizing ourselves with His written Word.

_____

_____

_____

_____

_____

_____

4. Let's make our focus true Christ-following.

_____

_____

_____

_____

_____

_____

5. Let's see the difficult things we face, not as evidence that God has abandoned us, but instead as the Shepherd rolling up His sleeves and moving to exert His will in making us more like Himself.

_____

_____

_____

_____

_____

_____

_____

Prayer

Heavenly Father,

Thank you for Your will. Thank You that it is not some secret, hidden agenda that I have to discover, some secret plan that I can miss out on if I make the wrong decisions. Thank You for revealing Your will for Your people in Your Word. Thank You, God, that You are not a micromanager, but a loving Shepherd. Help me to remember that in every decision I face, every choice I make.

Help me as I move ahead, Father, not to fall back into old ways of thinking. Don't let me believe the lie that I've missed Your will and my life is hopeless. Don't let me fret when I'm faced with a choice between two good options. Don't let me look for something outside of Your Word to direct and guide me. Help me to trust that You are good, and that Your Word is sufficient for teaching me Your will. Thank You for Your love and grace, and help me to trust You in all I say and do.

In the name of Jesus I pray, amen.